Eva Taylor

534-2625

T. McLemore
9-13-93

THE BAPTISM AND FULLNESS OF THE HOLY SPIRIT

other IVP books by John R. W. Stott

Basic Christianity

Basic Introduction to the New Testament

Men Made New

The Message of Galatians

Our Guilty Silence

THE BAPTISM AND FULLNESS
OF THE HOLY SPIRIT

John R. W. Stott

INTER-VARSITY PRESS

Downers Grove, Illinois 60515

*The substance of an address given
by the Rev. J. R. W. Stott
at the Islington Clerical Conference
on January 7, 1964 and
subsequently expanded for publication*

*© 1964
by Inter-Varsity Fellowship, England
Fifth American printing, April 1971
by Inter-Varsity Press
with permission from Inter-Varsity Fellowship*
*Inter-Varsity Press is the
book publishing division of
Inter-Varsity Christian Fellowship.*

ISBN 0-87784-421-6

Printed in the United States of America

the baptism and fullness of the Holy Spirit

It could almost be claimed that today the Holy Spirit is no longer what he has often been called, "the neglected Person in the Godhead." Certainly there is in our generation a welcome renewal of concern about his ministry in the Church and the world. There is also a recrudescence of "Pentecostalism" in non-Pentecostal churches, which rejoices some and bewilders or even alarms others. Christians of some years' standing are claiming to have received a "baptism of (or in) the Spirit" and to give evidence of it by "signs following." What can be said about these things?

The best way to begin is to stress the importance of our subject by confessing our great need of the power of the Holy Spirit today. We are ashamed of the general worldliness of the Church and disturbed by its weakness, its steadily diminishing influence on the country as a whole. Moreover, many of us are oppressed by our own personal failures in Christian life and Christian ministry.

We are conscious that we fall short both of the experience of the early Church and of the plain promises of God in his Word. We are thankful indeed for what God has done and is doing, and we do not want to denigrate his grace by minimizing it. But we hunger and thirst for more. We long for "revival," an altogether supernatural visitation of the Holy Spirit in the Church, and meanwhile for a deeper, richer, fuller experience of the Holy Spirit in our own lives.

As we approach this study, let me make three introductory points.

First, our common desire and duty as Christians are to enter into the full purpose of God; and this divine purpose is to be discerned in Scripture, not in the experience of particular individuals or groups, however true and valid these experiences may be. We should neither covet for ourselves what God may have given to others, nor urge upon others what God may have given to us, unless it is plainly revealed in his Word that this is part of the inheritance promised to all his people. What we see for ourselves and what we teach to others must be governed by the Scripture alone.

Secondly, this revelation of the purpose of God in Scripture should be sought in its *didactic,* rather than its *historical* parts. More precisely, we should look for it in the teaching of Jesus, and in the sermons and writings of the apostles, and not in the purely narrative portions of the Acts. What is *described* in Scripture as having happened to others is not necessarily intended for us, whereas what is *promised* to us we are to appropriate, and what is *commanded* us we are to obey.

Thirdly, our motive in thus seeking to discern God's purpose is practical and personal, not academic or controversial. We are brethren. We love one another. We are concerned to know God's will in order to embrace it ourselves and commend it to others, not in order to score cheap points off one another in theological debate.

After these three simple introductory points regarding our approach, let me bring you, from Scripture and in the light of some contemporary teaching, three major propositions about the individual Christian and the fullness of the Holy Spirit.

the Holy Spirit and the new age

First, *the fullness of the Holy Spirit is one of the distinctive blessings of the new age.* The new age is "the dispensation of the Spirit" (2 Cor. 3:8).[1] This is not, of course, to say that the Holy Spirit did not exist before, since he is God and therefore eternal. Nor is it to say that he was not active before. In Old Testament days he was ceaselessly active—in the creation and preservation of the universe, in providence and revelation, in the regeneration of believers, and in the equipment of special people for special tasks. Nevertheless, some of the prophets foretold that in the days of the Messiah God would grant a liberal effusion of the Holy Spirit, which would be new and distinctive, and available for all. Thus, Isaiah 32:15 speaks of the day when the Spirit will be "poured upon us from on high." In Isaiah 44:3 God promises: "I will pour water on the thirsty land, and streams on the dry ground; I will

[1]*Except where otherwise indicated, Scripture quotations are from the Revised Standard Version.*

11

pour my Spirit upon your descendants, and my blessings on your offspring." Again, in a better known passage, God says: "and it shall come to pass afterward, that I will pour out my spirit on all flesh" (Joel 2:28).

John the Baptist, the last prophet of the old order, summarized this expectation in his familiar saying which ascribed the outpouring of the Spirit to the Messiah himself: "I have baptized you with water; but he will baptize you with the Holy Spirit" (Mk. 1:8). Now it is of real importance to note that this prophecy of John recorded by the three Synoptic Evangelists as a simple future ("he will baptize"), takes the form in the Fourth Gospel of a present participle: "I myself did not know him; but he who sent me to baptize with water said to me, 'He on whom you see the Spirit descend and remain, this is he who baptizes with the Holy Spirit' " (Jn. 1:33). This use of the present participle is timeless. It describes not the single event of Pentecost, but the distinctive ministry of Jesus: "this is he who baptizes with the Holy Spirit."[2] Indeed, the very same words *ho baptizon,* which refer here to Jesus, are used by Mark to denote John the Baptist! Usually John is called *ho baptistes,* "the Baptist"; but three times in the narrative of Mark (1:4; 6:14, 24) he is called *ho baptizon,* an expression rendered in the RSV,

[2]*Another example of this Greek construction is in Gal. 1:23, where Saul of Tarsus is described as* ho diōkōn hēmas pote, *"he who once persecuted us," or simply "our former persecutor," indicating what was characteristic of him in his pre-conversion days.*

"the baptizer." In other words, just as John is called "the Baptist" or "the baptizer" because it was characteristic of his ministry to baptize with water, so Jesus is called "the Baptist" or "the baptizer," because it is characteristic of his ministry to baptize with the Holy Spirit.

This reference to the distinctive and continuing ministry of Jesus is strengthened by verse 29 of the same chapter (Jn. 1), in which the Baptist says, "Behold, the Lamb of God, who takes away the sin of the world." It is another present participle, *ho airon.* If we put verses 29 and 33 together, we discover that the characteristic work of Jesus is twofold. It involves a removal and a bestowal, a taking away of sin and a baptizing with the Holy Spirit. These are the two great gifts of Jesus Christ our Savior. They are brought together by the prophets in the Old Testament and the apostles in the New, and they cannot be separated. Thus, through the prophet Ezekiel God promised: "I will sprinkle clean water upon you, and you shall be clean. . . . And I will put my spirit within you, and cause you to walk in my statutes . . ." (36:25, 27). Similarly, the apostle Paul describes the new covenant as both "the dispensation of righteousness" and "the dispensation of the Spirit" (2 Cor. 3:9, 8). Again, Peter on the day of Pentecost cried: "Repent, and be baptized every one of you in the name of Jesus Christ for the forgiveness of your sins; and you shall receive the gift of the Holy Spirit" (Acts 2:38). The gift of the Spirit, as Peter here calls the baptism (*cf.* Acts 1:5), is as much an integral part

13

of the gospel of salvation as is the remission of sins. We must never conceive of salvation as the negative putting away of sins alone; it includes also the positive blessing of an indwelling Spirit. (See also Tit. 3:4-7.) When we repent and believe, Jesus not only takes away our sins, but also baptizes us with the Holy Spirit. Thus, the "baptism" or "gift" of the Spirit, which makes our experience of the fullness of the Holy Spirit possible, is one of the distinctive blessings of the new age.

Secondly, *the fullness of the Holy Spirit is not only a distinctive blessing of the new age, but a universal blessing.* The emphasis in the Joel prophecy, which Peter quoted on the day of Pentecost, is, "I will pour out my Spirit upon *all flesh.*" This cannot mean "all flesh" irrespective of their inward readiness to receive the gift, their repentance and faith, but rather "all flesh" irrespective of their outward status and privilege. It indicates that there is to be no distinction of sex or age, of rank or race, in the reception of this divine gift, for both sons and daughters, young men and old men, menservants and maidservants, and even "all that are far off" (Acts 2:39), which includes the Gentiles, are to receive it. Further, out of every age, sex, race, and rank it includes *all* who repent and believe. In Old Testament days, although all believers were indeed regenerate,[3] the Holy Spirit came upon

[3]*The chief evidences for this are indirect. First, they were certainly "justified" (cf. Rom. 4:1-8, based on Gen. 15:6 and Ps.*

special people for special ministries at special times. But now he is to come upon and to indwell all believers of all flesh.

That this was Peter's understanding of the prophecy of Joel is clear from the end of his great Pentecost sermon (Acts 2:38, 39) when he applied it to his hearers: "Repent, and be baptized every one of you in the name of Jesus Christ for the forgiveness of your sins; and you shall receive the gift of the Holy Spirit. For the promise (*i.e.* which we have inherited, see verse 33) is to you (as well as us) and to your children and to all that are far off, every one whom the Lord our God calls to him." This last phrase is a very clear and striking assertion. It is that the promise of the "gift" or "baptism" of the Spirit is to as many as the Lord our God calls. The promise of God is co-extensive with the call of God. Whoever receives the divine call inherits the divine promise.

And this is what happened! Three thousand of those who heard the word that day repented, believed and were

32:1, 2), and it is difficult to conceive how a sinner can be justified without being regenerate. Secondly, they claim to love God's law (e.g. Ps. 119:97). Since the unregenerate nature is hostile to God and resistant to his law (Rom. 8:7), they seem to have possessed a new nature. We sing the Psalms in Christian worship because we recognize in them the language of the regenerate. Nevertheless, it is plain from the promises of the prophets and of the Lord that there is an indwelling of the Spirit which they never knew and which belongs to the new covenant and to the kingdom of God (e.g. Ezek. 36:26, 27; Jn. 14:16, 17; Rom. 14:17).

baptized with water. And, although we are not specifically told that they received the remission of sins and the gift of the Spirit, yet the strong presumption is that they did, since Peter said they would if they repented, believed and were baptized. This means that, according to the second chapter of Acts, two separate companies of people received the "baptism" or "gift" of the Spirit on the day of Pentecost—the 120 at the beginning of the chapter, and the 3,000 at the end.

The 3,000 do not seem to have experienced the same miraculous phenomena (the rushing mighty wind, the tongues of flame, or speaking in other tongues). Yet they inherited the same promise and received the same gift (verses 33, 39). Nevertheless, there was this difference between them: the 120 were regenerate already, and only received the baptism of the Spirit after waiting upon God for ten days. The 3,000, on the other hand, were unbelievers and received the forgiveness of their sins and the gift of the Spirit simultaneously. And it happened immediately when they repented and believed; there was no necessity to wait. This distinction between the two companies, the 120 and the 3,000, is of great importance, because I suggest that the *norm* for Christian experience today is the second group, the 3,000, and not (as is often supposed) the first. The fact that the experience of the 120 was in two distinct stages was simply due to historical circumstances. They could not have received the Pentecostal gift before Pentecost. But on and after the day of

Pentecost forgiveness of sins and the "gift" or "baptism" of the Spirit were received together.

Some readers will immediately object that the 120 were not unique, since the experience of certain Samaritan believers and of some disciples of John the Baptist, recorded later in the Acts (8:5-17 and 19:1-7), was in two stages also. In answer to this common objection, I must first repeat that a doctrine of the Holy Spirit must not be constructed from descriptive passages in the Acts. It would be impossible to build a consistent doctrine from them because there is no consistency about them. You cannot even derive a doctrine of the Holy Spirit from the *description* of the day of Pentecost; what I have attempted above is some deductions from the *interpretations* of the event which Peter gave in his sermon. Further, it is a fundamental principle of biblical interpretation to begin with the general, not the special. If it be asked what the general teaching of the New Testament is regarding the reception of the Holy Spirit, we can give a plain and definite answer: we receive the Holy Spirit "by hearing (*sc.* the gospel) with faith" (Gal. 3:2) or, more simply still, "through faith" (Gal. 3:14). As a result, all God's sons possess the Spirit (Gal. 4:6), are led by the Spirit (Rom. 8:14), and are assured by the Spirit of their sonship and of God's love (Rom. 8:15, 16; 5:5), while those who do not possess the Spirit do not belong to Christ at all (Rom. 8:9; Jude 19).

If now we look carefully at the Acts 8 and 19 passages

mentioned above, we shall not fail to observe that there is something unusual about both situations. The twelve men whom Paul met in Ephesus (Acts 19:1-7) do not seem to have been Christians at all. It is true that they are called "disciples," but the story reveals that they were actually disciples of John the Baptist. It is true also that Paul asked them if they received the Holy Spirit when they believed (verse 2), indicating that he at first thought they were believers. But their reply to his question and what followed suggest that he was mistaken. Note these points: they had never even heard of the Holy Spirit (verse 2); they had to be told that "the one who was to come," in whom John had told them to believe, was in fact Jesus (verse 4); and Paul not only laid hands on them but had first to baptize them into "the name of the Lord Jesus" (verse 5). Can those who have never heard of the Holy Spirit, nor been baptized into Christ, nor even apparently believed in him, be called Christians? I think not. These disciples of John certainly cannot be made typical of the average Christian believer today.

This leaves Acts 8:5-17. Here Philip had preached the gospel in Samaria, and many had believed and been baptized. There can be no question but that they were Christian believers.[4] But what is plainly unusual about

---

[4]*Simon Magus was an exception. He is said to have "believed" (verse 13), but his profession of faith turned out to be spurious (verses 20-23).*

this incident is that "when the apostles at Jerusalem heard that Samaria had received the Word of God, they sent to them Peter and John" (verse 14). Why? There is no evidence that on other occasions evangelistic work had to be inspected by two apostles. For example, at the end of the same chapter (verses 26-40) the same Philip preached the gospel to an Ethiopian eunuch and baptized him when he believed. But no apostle was sent to investigate or to lay hands on him. What then is the explanation of this unusual procedure of an apostolic delegation?

The most likely answer is not just that this was the first time the gospel had been preached outside Jerusalem (verses 1, 4), but that these converts were Samaritans and in those days Jews had "no dealings with Samaritans" (Jn. 4:9). Their rivalry had lasted for centuries and might well have survived in the Church in a disastrous division between Jewish Christians and Samaritan Christians. May it not have been in order to avoid a perpetuation of this schism that God deliberately withheld the gift of his Spirit from the Samaritan believers until two of the leading apostles came down to investigate and, by the laying on of their hands, acknowledged and confirmed the genuineness of the Samaritans' conversion? Certainly this passage gives no more warrant for the "Pentecostal" view that the Holy Spirit is given subsequently to conversion than for the "Catholic" view that he is given only through the imposition of the apostolic hands. We must insist that both the timing and the means of the gift were atypical;

neither a two-stage experience nor the laying on of hands is the norm for receiving the Spirit today.[5]

After this excursus into chapters 8 and 19 of the Acts, let us revert to chapter 2. What has emerged from our study of this chapter, and is not negatived by the exceptional cases in Acts 8 and 19, is that the "gift" or "baptism" of the Spirit is a *universal* Christian experience because it is an *initial* Christian experience. This is the general teaching of the New Testament. To be "in the Spirit" (which in Pauline language is equivalent to being "in Christ"), to "have" the Spirit, to "live by the Spirit" and be "led by the Spirit"—these are all descriptions of every Christian believer (Rom. 8:9; Gal. 5:25; Rom. 8:14). The New Testament authors take it for granted that God has "given" their readers his Holy Spirit (*e.g.* Rom. 5:5; 1 Thess. 4:8; 1 Jn. 3:24; 4:13); they never exhort them to receive him.

This truth is further confirmed by the New Testament use of the expression to "baptize" or "be baptized" with the Holy Spirit, which we must now consider. To begin

[5]*Episcopal "Confirmation" is the way the Anglican Church has chosen to receive into full church membership those who have been baptized (usually in infancy) and have themselves repented and believed. The laying on of hands is a seemly biblical sign of blessing, but is not the normal means by which the Holy Spirit is given and received. The 1662 Book of Common Prayer implies no more than that God may use this sign, accompanied by the prayers of the congregation, to "certify" the candidates of his favor towards them and to "strengthen" them by the Holy Spirit.*

with, the very concept of "baptism" is initiatory. Water-baptism is the rite of initiation into Christ. It is the symbol of which Spirit-baptism is the reality. This is why Peter's immediate reaction, when Cornelius was baptized with the Spirit, was: "Can anyone forbid water for baptizing these people who have received the Holy Spirit just as we have?" (Acts 10:47; 11:16) If they had received the reality, how could they be denied the sign?

This idea of initiation is further established when we compare the seven verses in which baptism with the Spirit is specifically mentioned. Four of them record the prophecy of John the Baptist in the Gospels (Mt. 3:11; Mk. 1:8; Lk. 3:16; Jn. 1:33). The fifth is our Lord's quotation of it (Acts 1:5), in which he applies it to Pentecost. The sixth is in Acts 11:16, where Peter quotes our Lord's quotation of John the Baptist, and applies it to the conversion of Cornelius. The seventh is in 1 Corinthians 12. What the apostle is doing in this passage, before unfolding the *diversity* of spiritual gifts, is to emphasize the *unity* of the Spirit, the giver. He is stressing our common experience, as Christian brethren, of the Holy Spirit. Three times he writes (literally) of "the one Spirit" (9b, 13a and b), three times of "the same Spirit" (4, 8, 9a), and once of the "one and the same Spirit" (11). This is his emphasis. His climax comes in verse 13: "For by one Spirit we were all baptized into one body . . . and all were made to drink of one Spirit." So the baptism of the Spirit in this verse, far from being a dividing factor (some have it, others have not), is the great uniting factor (an experience we have all had). It is, in fact, the means of entry into the body of Christ, and Paul's mention of Jews and Greeks, slaves and free, seems to be an allusion to Joel's "all flesh" irrespective of race or rank. The oneness of the body is created by the oneness of the Spirit. (*Cf.* Eph. 4:3, 4.) It is difficult to resist the conclusion that the baptism of the Spirit is not a second and subsequent experience, enjoyed by some Christians, but the initial experience enjoyed by all.

Some seek to escape the implication of this verse by drawing a subtle exegetical distinction. They argue that, while the other six verses refer to a baptism by Jesus Christ in or with the Holy Spirit, the seventh verse (1 Cor. 12:13) refers to a baptism by the Holy Spirit into the body of Christ, and is therefore something quite different. "The Holy Spirit has indeed baptized us all into the body of Christ," they say, "but this does not prove that Christ has baptized us all with the Holy Spirit." I must respectfully say that this is special pleading. The Greek expression is precisely the same in all its seven occurrences,[6] and therefore *a priori,* as a sound principle of interpretation, it should refer to the same baptism experience in each verse. The burden of proof rests with those who deny it. The natural interpretation is that Paul is echoing the words of John the Baptist as first Jesus and

[6] *The only difference is that six times the Spirit is characterized as "holy," and in the seventh verse as "one."*

then Peter had done (Acts 1:5; 11:16). It is unwarrantable to make Jesus Christ the baptizer in six instances, and the Holy Spirit the baptizer in the seventh. We must even dissent from the RSV translation of 1 Corinthians 12:13, "*by* one Spirit we were all baptized . . . ." The Greek preposition in this verse is *en*, just as in the other six verses, where it is translated "with"; why should it be rendered differently here? If it is because the words *en heni pneumati* (RSV, "by one Spirit") come at the beginning of the sentence, the reason for this is surely that Paul is stressing the oneness of the Spirit in whom we share, not that the Spirit is the baptizer.

Let me enlarge on my point in this way. In every kind of baptism (of water, blood, fire, Spirit, *etc.*) there are four parts. To begin with, there are the subject and the object, namely the baptizer and the baptized. Thirdly, there is the element with or in (*en*) which, and fourthly, there is the purpose for (*eis*) which, the baptism takes place. Take, as an example, the crossing of the Red Sea, which the apostle Paul describes as a baptism (1 Cor. 10:1, 2). Presumably God himself was the baptizer. Certainly, the escaping Israelites were the baptized. The element in which the baptism was administered was water from the cloud and the sea, while its purpose is indicated in the expression "baptized into Moses," that is, into relationship to him as their God-appointed leader.

In John's baptism, John the Baptist was the subject, while the objects were the people of "Jerusalem and all

Judea and all the region about the Jordan" (Mt. 3:5). The baptism took place in (*en*) the waters of the River Jordan and was for, or unto (*eis*), repentance (Mt. 3:11) and therefore the remission of sins (Mk. 1:4; Lk. 3:3). Christian baptism is similar. The minister baptizes the professing believer with, or in (*en*), water, into (*eis*) the one name of the Trinity (Mt. 28:19), or more precisely, into the name of the Lord Jesus (Acts 8:16; 19:5), that is, into Christ crucified and risen (Rom. 6:3, 4).

It will be seen from these examples that in every kind of baptism there are not only a subject and an object, but also both an *en* and an *eis*, that is, both an element with or in which, and a purpose for which, the baptism is administered. The baptism of the Spirit is no exception. If we put the seven references to this baptism together, we learn that Jesus Christ is the baptizer, as John the Baptist clearly foretold. According to 1 Corinthians 12:13 the baptized are "we all" (AV). The Holy Spirit is himself the "element" with, or in (*en*), which[7] the baptism takes

---

[7]*Pentecostalists usually speak of "baptism in the Spirit" rather than "baptism with the Spirit." The Greek preposition en may be translated either way. The expression chosen is likely to depend on whether one considers that water-baptism should be administered by immersion or by affusion. Those who practice immersion speak of baptism in the Spirit presumably because they think of the Spirit as the element in which one is plunged. Since it is when the Holy Spirit is "poured out" upon people that they are said to be "baptized," however, "baptism with the Spirit" is preferable.*

place (if one may so describe the third person of the Trinity; the analogy between baptism with water and baptism with the Spirit seems to make it legitimate). And the purpose of this baptism is incorporation "into (*eis*) one body," namely the body of Christ, the Church.

It is quite true that of these four aspects of baptism the only one which is explicitly common to all seven verses is that this baptism is "with (*en*) the Spirit." Although all thus mention the "element," not every verse specifies either the subject or the object or the purpose of the baptism. This should not surprise us, however, since the same omissions occur with New Testament references to water-baptism. It cannot be argued that in 1 Corinthians 12:13 the Holy Spirit must be the baptizer—since otherwise the baptism would have no subject—for no baptizer is mentioned in Acts 1:5 and 11:16 either. Yet we find no difficulty in supplying Jesus Christ as the baptizer in those verses, and we should do the same in 1 Corinthians 12:13. The reason why Christ is not specifically mentioned as the baptizer in these three verses is not far to seek. It is that, whereas in the four Gospels' verses the verb is in the active and Christ is its subject ("he will baptize," "this is he who baptizes"), in these other three verses the verb is passive and the subject is those baptized ("you shall be baptized," "we were all baptized"). Because these verbs are passive, the identity of the baptizer fades, and the emphasis lies rather on either the favored people who receive the baptism or the one Spirit with whom they are baptized. I would, therefore, reaffirm that in 1 Corinthians 12:13, although he is not named, Jesus Christ must be regarded as the baptizer.

The argument rests partly on the six other verses in which the same expression occurs and partly on the impossibility of the alternative. If 1 Corinthians 12:13 were different and in this verse the Holy Spirit were himself the baptizer, what would be the "element" with which he baptizes? That there is no answer to this question is enough to overthrow this interpretation, since the baptism metaphor absolutely requires an "element," or the baptism is no baptism. Therefore, the "element" in the baptism of 1 Corinthians 12:13 must be the Holy Spirit, and (consistently with the other verses) we must supply Jesus Christ as the baptizer. Similarly, at the end of the verse it is the Holy Spirit of whom we drink, and consistently (with Jn. 7:37 ff.) it must be Christ by whom we are "made to drink" of him.

The importance of establishing that 1 Corinthians 12:13 refers to Christ baptizing with the Spirit and causing us to drink of the Spirit is that "we all" have shared in this baptism and this drinking. The being baptized and the drinking are clearly equivalent expressions. All Christians have experienced them both. Moreover, the aorist tense of both verbs ("were . . . baptized," "were made to drink") must be taken as an allusion, not just to the Pentecost event, but also to its blessing personally received by all Christians at their conversion.

27

The evidence, then, which we have sought to gather from the New Testament in general, and in particular from Peter's sermon in Acts 2 and Paul's teaching in 1 Corinthians 12:13, indicates that the "gift" or "baptism" of the Spirit, one of the *distinctive* blessings of the new covenant, is a *universal* blessing for members of the covenant, because it is an *initial* blessing. It is part and parcel of belonging to the new age. The Lord Jesus, the mediator of the new covenant and the bestower of its blessings, gives both the forgiveness of sins and the gift of the Spirit to all who enter his covenant. Further, baptism with water is the sign and seal of baptism with the Spirit, as much as it is of the forgiveness of sins. Water-baptism is the initiatory Christian rite, because Spirit-baptism is the initiatory Christian experience.

God's norm, therefore, for all his people is first to receive the new covenant blessing of the forgiveness of sins and the gift of the Spirit, then to receive water-baptism as the sign and seal of these blessings, and then to continue to be filled with the Spirit and to manifest this fullness in holiness of life and boldness of testimony. All Christians are described in the Epistle to the Hebrews as being "partakers of the Holy Spirit," who have "tasted . . . the powers of the age to come" (6:4, 5). The whole Christian life according to the New Testament is life in the Spirit following birth of the Spirit. Moreover, the overwhelming emphasis of the New Testament epistles is not to urge upon Christian readers some entirely new and distinct blessing, but to remind us of what by grace we are and to recall us to it. The possibility and necessity of holiness, according to the First Epistle of John, are ascribed not to a special "baptism of the Spirit" which we have had or should have, but to our original birth of God (*e.g.* 2:29; 3:9, 10; 5:18) and to our "abiding" in him (2:6, 28; 3:6; *cf.* Jn. 15:1 ff.).

If someone impatiently objects that surely this is merely a verbal quibble, and does it really matter, we would reply that the argument is not about words, but about theology. The fundamental doctrine we are seeking to establish is that by uniting us to Christ God has given us everything, and that there is nothing new to follow except the resurrection and glorification of our bodies. By God's unutterable grace we have already been "blessed . . . in Christ with every spiritual blessing" (Eph. 1:3), and our responsibility is constantly and progressively to appropriate these blessings which are already ours in Christ. Thus, we are born of God, his sons and heirs, dead and risen with Christ, and indwelt by the Spirit, who is the earnest of our heavenly inheritance. And what the New Testament authors do is constantly to remind us of our Christian status and privileges, in order to exhort us to walk worthy of the vocation with which we have been called.

Thirdly, as has just been anticipated, *the fullness of the Holy Spirit,* which we have seen to be a distinctive and universal blessing of the new covenant, *is also a continuous blessing, to be continuously and increasingly appropriated.* Having asserted this, let me refer you at once to some stirring words of Jesus which are recorded in John 7:37-39 and which have been (and remain) a great help to me: "On the last day of the feast, the great day, Jesus stood up and proclaimed, 'If any one thirst, let him come to me and drink. He who believes in me, as the scripture has said, "Out of his heart shall flow rivers of living water." ' Now this," John comments, "he said about the Spirit, which those who believed in him were to receive; for as yet the Spirit had not been given, because Jesus was not yet glorified." "It has been said," wrote Bishop J. C. Ryle, "that there are some passages in Scripture which deserve to be printed in letters of Gold. Of such passages the verses before us form one." It was the last day of the Feast of the Tabernacles (verse 2), the climax of its seven days. One of the colorful rituals of the festival was that every morning a solemn procession, headed by a priest carrying a golden pitcher, went to fetch water from the Pool of Siloam and then poured it out as a libation on the west side of the altar. It was generally understood, I have been told, that this ceremony not only commemorated God's miraculous provision in the wilderness, but also symbolized the future outpouring of the Spirit promised through the prophet Joel. Jesus took this ritual as his text. He stood forth dramatically in some prominent place (he usually sat to teach like the rabbis), and loudly proclaimed that he himself would give to those who came to him both water to drink and water to flow.

What did he mean? He combined two vivid pictures. The first is of a tired and thirsty traveler in a hot climate. The sun beats down mercilessly upon him. His water supply has run out. His mouth is dry, his lips parched, his face flushed, his whole body dehydrated. He pants for water to quench his thirst. He represents every person who is separated in any degree from Christ. The second picture is of a thirsty land. The tropical sun has baked the ground hard. The river beds are dry. Trees and shrubs are shrivelled. Animals groan because there is no pasture. The land thirsts for water. This is the world, secular society without God, desiccated, dissatisfied, thirsty.

What, then, is the water? John tells us: "This he said about the Spirit." And John adds that "as yet the Spirit had not been given." His actual words, literally translated, are "the Spirit was not yet." This can mean neither that the Spirit was non-existent nor that he was inactive, but that he had not yet been poured out in Pentecostal fullness, in "rivers of living water." So the living water to quench the thirst of the weary traveler and to irrigate the parched world is the fullness of the Holy Spirit.

And how do we experience this invigorating, refreshing, thirstquenching fullness? The answer is: "Let him come to me and drink. He who believes in me . . . ." The phrases are two, but the condition is one. There is no difference between coming to Jesus and believing in him, for coming to him implies faith. Now the verbs (thirsting, coming, drinking, believing) are all in the present tense. We are to keep coming, to keep drinking, because we keep thirsting. We do this physically. Whenever we are thirsty, we get a drink. We must learn to do it spiritually also. The Christian is a spiritual dipsomaniac, always thirsty, always drinking. And drinking is not asking for water, but actually taking it. It is so simple. Drinking is one of the first activities we learn.

Then drinking water becomes flowing water. We cannot contain the Spirit we receive. As William Temple wrote: "No one can possess (or rather be indwelt by) the Spirit of God and keep that Spirit to himself. Where the Spirit is, He flows forth; if there is no flowing forth, He is not there." We must beware of any claim to the fullness of the Spirit which does not lead to an evangelistic concern and outreach. Moreover, notice the disparity between the water we drink in and the water that flows out. We can only drink small gulps, but as we keep coming, drinking, believing, the mighty operation of the Holy Spirit within us produces a river of living water. This is the spontaneous outflow from Spirit-filled Christians to the blessing of others. But there is no button to press in order to settle this issue for good. There is no way to ensure a constant inflow and a constant outflow, except to keep coming to Jesus and to keep drinking, for the fullness of the Spirit is to be continuously appropriated.

To grasp this great truth is to anticipate a common objection. The chief argument against the interpretation of the baptism of the Spirit which I have given above is not biblical but empirical, not theoretical but practical. It could be stated in two sentences: (1) If all Christians have been baptized with the Spirit, the majority do not appear to have been! (2) Some Christians claim to have received a further and distinct experience of the Holy Spirit, and *their* claim does appear to be true!

I would tentatively explain these phenomena thus: Although all Christians have indeed been baptized with the Holy Spirit, many of us live on a level lower than our Spirit-baptism makes possible, because we do not remain filled with the Holy Spirit, while some are given further, exceptional experience apart from their initial reception of the Spirit. Let us examine this suggested explanation of these two groups of people.

We shall take first what may be called the "average" Christian today. Can it really be maintained, we are asked, that he has been baptized with the Spirit? Two problems lie behind the question. They concern his conversion and his subsequent life. His conversion, it is said, was quite unspectacular and not at all like a baptism of the Spirit, while his present Christian life supplies no evidence of his having been thus baptized. The denial that Christian conversion today is or includes a baptism with the Spirit depends on an *a priori* assumption regarding what a baptism with the Spirit is like. All the time people have the events of the day of Pentecost at the back of their minds. They forget that the supernatural signs associated with Pentecost are no more typical of every baptism of the Spirit than those on the Damascus road are of every conversion. The wind and the fire at Pentecost, like the light and the voice on the Damascus road, were the dramatic outward accompaniments; they were no neces-

35

sary part of the essential inward experience. What biblical warrant is there for supposing that people cannot receive the "gift" or "baptism" of the Spirit in a quiet and unsensational way?

Next, what about the low level at which the average Christian lives today? Can it really be claimed that he has been baptized with the Spirit? Let us consider this subsidiary question. I am certainly not wishing to deny or excuse the sub-normality of much of our Christian living today. It is often true and very sad. Our sins and unbelief have robbed many of us of our full inheritance. We need to repent and return to God. But the backslidings of Christians are evidence of their need, not to be baptized with the Spirit (even the proud, loveless, quarrelsome and sin-tolerant Corinthian Christians had been baptized with the Spirit; see 1 Cor. 12:13), but to recover the fullness of the Spirit which they have lost through sin, thus becoming what the Corinthian Christians were, namely "unspiritual" or "carnal" (1 Cor. 3:1 ff.). It is in this sense that many Christians do have an experience in two stages or more. It is not the general will and purpose of God (which is a continuous and increasing appropriation); it is due rather to their sinful backsliding.

Let me seek to elaborate this. What happened on the day of Pentecost was that Jesus "poured out" the Spirit from heaven and thus "baptized" with the Spirit first the 120 and then the 3,000. The result of this baptism of the Spirit was (Acts 2:4) that "they were all filled with the

Holy Spirit." Thus, the fullness of the Spirit was the consequence of the baptism of the Spirit. The baptism is what Jesus did (pouring out the Spirit from heaven); the fullness is what they received. The baptism was a unique initiatory experience; the fullness was intended to be the continuing, the permanent result, the norm. (See Acts 6:3; 7:55; 11:24; 13:52 and Lk. 1:15, 41, 67.) As an initiatory event the baptism is not repeatable and cannot be lost, but the filling can be repeated and in any case needs to be maintained. If it is not maintained, it is lost. If it is lost, it can be recovered. The Holy Spirit is "grieved" by sin (Eph. 4:30) and ceases to fill the sinner. Repentance is then the only road to recovery. Even in cases where there is no suggestion that the fullness has been forfeited through sin, we still read of people being filled again, as a fresh crisis or challenge demands a fresh empowering by the Spirit. Thus, we read in Acts 4:8 of Peter being again filled with the Holy Spirit, and in Acts 4:31 of the whole company being again filled. There is a similar double reference to an infilling in relation to Paul (Acts 9:17; 13:9), while Ephesians 5:18 contains the well-known command to all Christian people to be filled, that is, to go on being filled (a continuous present imperative) with the Spirit.

There are no similar statements or commands in the New Testament about the baptism of the Spirit, because of its initiatory character. No apostolic sermon or epistle contains an appeal to be baptized with the Spirit. Indeed, all seven New Testament references to baptism with the Spirit are in the indicative, whether aorist, present, or future; none is an exhortation in the imperative. But these references to the fullness of the Spirit, both describing how certain Christians were filled and exhorting others to be filled, show that it is possible, and all too pitifully common, for Christians who have been baptized with the Spirit to cease to be filled with the Spirit.

The Corinthian Christians are a solemn warning to us on this score. It is plain from Paul's first letter to them that they had been baptized, all of them, with the Holy Spirit (12:13). They had also been enriched with all spiritual gifts (1:4-7). Yet the apostle rebukes them as *unspiritual* people, that is, as being not Spirit-filled. He makes it clear that the evidence of the Spirit's fullness is not the exercise of his gifts (of which they had plenty), but the ripening of his fruit (of which they had little). (See Gal. 5:22, 23.) He could not address them, he writes, as *pneumatikoi,* "spiritual" Christians, but as *sarkinoi* or *sarkikoi,* "carnal" Christians, even babes in Christ. Their carnality or immaturity was both intellectual and moral. It was revealed in their childish understanding on the one hand and in their jealousy and strife on the other (1 Cor. 3:1-4). They had been *baptized* with the Spirit, and richly *gifted* by the Spirit, but they were not (at least at the time of his visit and letter to them) *filled* with the Spirit. The apostle's distinction, you notice, is not between those who have received the baptism of the Spirit and those who have not, but between Christians filled with the Spirit ("spiritual") and those dominated by the flesh ("carnal"). Leaving aside the question of gifts (which is not my subject) is not the condition of these Corinthians the state of many of us today? We cannot deny that, according to Scripture, we have been baptized with the Spirit because we have repented and believed, and our water-baptism has signified and sealed our Spirit-baptism. But are we filled with the Spirit? That is the question.

Many people would be unable to answer this question. They know neither whether they are filled with the Spirit nor how it is possible to tell. And when they come across Pentecostal teaching that "speaking in tongues" is the indispensable sign of having received the Spirit, they conclude that they have never received him, or at least his fullness. But it cannot be maintained from Scripture that "tongues" always follows the reception of the Spirit. Of all the groups who received the Spirit in the book of Acts only three are said to have spoken in tongues (2:1-4; 10:44-46; 19:1-6). Since the other people and groups who received the Spirit are not said to have spoken in tongues, it is quite arbitrary to assert that they did. Besides, the apostle categorically teaches in 1 Corinthians 12 that the gift of tongues is only one of many gifts which not all believers are given; and there is no solid foundation for the Pentecostalist distinction between the references to "tongues" in Acts and those in 1 Corinthians 12, 14, the former referring to the "sign" of tongues which all must have and the latter to the "gift" of tongues which only some receive. Indeed, several leading Pentecostalist pastors are themselves now conceding that "tongues" is not an indispensable sign of the gift of the Spirit.

What then is the evidence of the Spirit's indwelling and fullness? As with the baptism, so with the fullness, the chief evidence is moral, not miraculous. It consists of the fruit of the Spirit, not the gifts of the Spirit. We have already seen that the Corinthians, who had been baptized with the Spirit, gave evidence of being "unspiritual" Christians by their lack of the moral quality of love (1 Cor. 3:1-4). More positively, in the one and only passage in his epistles in which the apostle Paul describes the consequences of the Spirit's fullness, they are all moral qualities.[8] This passage is Ephesians 5:18-21 and we must consider it carefully. "And do not get drunk with wine, for that is debauchery; but be filled with the Spirit, addressing one another in psalms and hymns and spiritual songs, singing and making melody to the Lord with all your heart, always and for everything giving thanks in the name of our Lord Jesus Christ to God the Father. Be subject to one another out of reverence for Christ." In the Greek text this paragraph consists of two verbs in the imperative ("do not get drunk with wine ... but be filled with the Spirit"), on which depend four verbs which are

[8] *"The fruit of the Spirit" in Gal. 5:22, 23 consists of moral qualities too, and by fruit is meant the natural produce of a life lived in the Spirit.*

present participles (literally "speaking," "singing and making melody," "giving thanks," and "submitting"). That is, the single command to be filled with the Spirit is followed by four descriptive consequences of the Holy Spirit's fullness.

The command to be filled is placed in vivid contrast to the other command not to get drunk. Some people have too readily deduced from this that the fullness of the Spirit is a kind of spiritual inebriation, and what the apostle is doing is to set over against each other two intoxicated states, physical through wine and spiritual through the Spirit's fullness. This is not so. It is true that on the day of Pentecost, when the 120 spoke publicly in other tongues as the Spirit gave them utterance, the crowd's reaction was to comment, "they are filled with new wine" (Acts 2:13). But it is a mistake to suppose that their ecstatic state is intended to be a pattern for all future experience of the Spirit's fullness, any more than are the rushing mighty wind and the tongues of flame. Besides, there is a clear implication in Ephesians 5:18 that drunkenness and the Spirit's fullness are not comparable in this respect, for drunkenness is branded as "excess" (AV) or "debauchery" (RSV). The Greek word *asōtia,* which in its two other New Testament occurrences means "profligacy" (Tit. 1:6; 1 Pet. 4:4), literally describes a condition in which a person cannot "save" or control himself. It is because drunkenness involves a loss of self-control, Paul writes, that it is to be avoided. It is implied that the contrasting state, the fullness of the Spirit, involves no loss of self-control. On the contrary, we are distinctly told in Galatians 5:23 that a part of the fruit of the Spirit is self-control (*enkrateia*)! The consequences of the fullness of the Spirit, as the apostle goes on to portray them, are to be found in intelligent, controlled, healthy relationships with God and with each other. We can indeed agree that the contrast between drunkenness and the fullness of the Spirit implies two strong and different influences at work within us, alcohol in the bloodstream and the Holy Spirit in our hearts. But, whereas excessive alcohol leads to unrestrained and irrational license, transforming the drunkard into an animal, the fullness of the Spirit leads to restrained and rational moral behavior, transforming the Christian into the image of Christ. Thus, the results of being under the influence of spirits on the one hand and of the Holy Spirit of God on the other are totally and utterly different. One makes us like beasts, the other like Christ.

marks of the fullness of the Spirit

We are now in a position to look at the four wholesome results, and thereby solid, objective evidences, of the fullness of the Spirit (Eph. 5:18-20). These results are seen in relationships. The Spirit's fullness involves not a private, mystical experience so much as moral relationships with God and our fellow men. The first is "speaking." According to the AV, it is "speaking to yourselves." This does not mean that those who are filled with the Spirit start talking to themselves as if their minds had become unhinged! The RSV is certainly correct in rendering the expression "addressing one another." Compare the parallel passage, Colossians 3:16. It is very striking that the first evidence of being filled with the Spirit is that we speak to each other. Yet it is not surprising, since the first-fruit of the Spirit is love. However deep and intimate our communion with God may seem, we cannot claim the fullness of the Spirit if we are not on speaking terms with any of our fellows. The first sign of fullness is fellowship. Moreover, it is a spiritual fellowship, for we address one another not in worldly chitchat but in "psalms and hymns and spiritual songs." This cannot of course mean that the normal method of communication between Spirit-filled believers is song! It means rather that true fellowship is expressed in common worship. A good example is the *Venite* (Ps. 95), which Anglicans sing in public worship every Sunday morning. Strictly speaking, it is not a psalm of worship at all, since it is not addressed to God but to the congregation: "O come, let us sing unto the Lord." Here are God's people addressing one another in a psalm, exhorting one another to worship their Lord.

This leads to the second result of the Spirit's fullness, which is "singing and making melody" to the Lord. The Holy Spirit loves to glorify the Lord Jesus, so manifesting him to his people that they delight to sing his praises. Unmusical people have sometimes taken comfort from this exhortation to sing to the Lord "in your hearts" (AV), as if their jubilation could be entirely inward, intended only "for the ears of the Lord" (J. B. Phillips). But the RSV is probably right to translate the expression "with all your heart." The heart is not so much the place as the manner in which we are to sing. The apostle exhorts us not to silence, but to heartfelt worship.

Thirdly, we are to be "always and for everything giving thanks." Most of us give thanks sometimes for some things; Spirit-filled believers give thanks always for all things. There is no time at which, and no circumstances for which, they do not give thanks. They do so "in the name of our Lord Jesus Christ," that is, because they are one with Christ, and "to God the Father," because the Holy Spirit witnesses with their spirit that they are God's children and that their Father is wholly good and wise. Grumbling, one of Israel's besetting sins, is serious because it is a symptom of unbelief. Whenever we start moaning and groaning, it is proof positive that we are not filled with the Spirit. Whenever the Holy Spirit fills believers, they thank their Heavenly Father at all times for all things.

We have seen that the second and third marks of the Spirit's fullness are both Godward—singing to the Lord and giving thanks to the Father. The Holy Spirit puts us into a right and praising relationship with the Father and the Son. The Spirit-filled believer has no practical difficulties with the doctrine of the Trinity. The first and fourth marks, however, concern our relationship with each other, speaking to one another and now submitting to one another. Although the apostle goes on to show that submission is the *particular* duty of a wife to her husband, children to their parents and servants to their masters, he begins by making it the *general* duty of all Christians to each other (including husbands, parents and masters). Humble submission is such an important part of Christian behavior that the verb occurs 32 times in the New Testament. Not self-assertion but self-submission, is the hallmark of the Spirit-filled Christian. Sometimes, it is true, when a fundamental theological or moral principle is at stake, we must not give way, as when Paul withstood Peter to the face at Antioch; but we must always beware lest our supposed stand on principle is in reality an ugly exhibition of pride. It is wise to distrust our righteous indignation; there is usually more than a smattering of unrighteous vanity in it. The test is in the last words of the sentence: "out of reverence for Christ." Our first duty is reverent and humble submission to the Lord Christ. We should submit to others right up to the point where our submission to them would mean disloyalty to Christ.

The wholesome results of the fullness of the Spirit are now laid bare. The two chief spheres in which this fullness is manifest are worship and fellowship. If we are filled with the Spirit, we shall be praising Christ and thanking our Father, and speaking and submitting to one another. The Holy Spirit puts us in a right relationship with both God and man. It is in these spiritual qualities and activities, not in supernatural phenomena, that we should look for evidence of the Holy Spirit's fullness. This is the apostle's emphasis when he is dealing with the subject in the Corinthian, Galatian and Ephesian epistles.

We now come back to the command, upon which depend the four present participles which we have been considering: "be filled with the Spirit." Notice these three points. First, it is a plural verb. Both imperatives in Ephesians 5:18, the prohibition and the command, are universal in their application. We are none of us to get drunk; we are all of us to be Spirit-filled. The fullness of the Spirit is emphatically not a privilege reserved for the few, but a duty resting upon all. The Holy Spirit's fullness, like sobriety and self-control, is obligatory, not optional. Secondly, it is a passive verb: "be filled." That is, "let the Holy Spirit fill you" (NEB). An important condition of enjoying his fullness is to yield to him without reserve. Nevertheless, it must not be imagined that we are purely passive agents in receiving the Spirit's fullness, any more than in getting drunk. A man gets drunk by drinking; we become filled with the Spirit by drinking too, as we have already seen from our Lord's teaching in John 7:37, ". . . come to me and drink."

Thirdly, the verb is in the present tense. It is well known that in the Greek language, if the imperative is aorist it refers to a single action, while if it is present the action is continuous. Thus, when at the wedding in Cana Jesus said, "fill the jars with water" (Jn. 2:7), the aorist imperative shows that he meant them to do it once only. The present imperative "be filled with the Spirit," on the other hand, indicates not some dramatic or decisive experience which will settle the issue for good, but a continuous appropriation. This is further enforced in the epistle to the Ephesians by the contrast between the "sealing" and the "filling" of the Spirit. Twice the apostle writes that his readers have been "sealed" with the Holy Spirit (Eph. 1:13, 4:30). The aorists are identical and describe every penitent believer. God has accepted him and placed upon him the seal of the Spirit, to authenticate him, to mark him, and to secure him as his own. But although all believers are "sealed," not all believers remain "filled," for the sealing is past and finished, while the filling is (or should be) present and continuous.

Perhaps an illustration will help at this point to show that the fullness of the Spirit is intended to be not a static but a developing experience. Let us compare two people. One is a baby, newborn and weighing 7 lbs.—who has just begun to breathe; the other is a full-grown man, six feet in height and 168 lbs. in weight. Both are fit and healthy; both are breathing properly; and both may be described as "filled with air." What, then, is the difference between them? It lies in the capacity of their lungs. Both are "filled," yet one is more filled than the other because his capacity is greater. Let us apply this to spiritual life and growth. Who will deny that a newborn babe in Christ is filled with the Spirit? The body of every believer is the temple of the Holy Spirit (1 Cor. 6:19); are we to suppose that, when the Spirit enters his temple, he does not fill it? A mature and godly Christian of many years' standing is filled with the Spirit also. The difference between them is to be found in what might be called their spiritual lung capacity, namely the measure of their grasp of God's purpose for them. This is clear from the apostle's prayer for the Ephesian Christians "that the God of our Lord Jesus Christ, the Father of glory, may give you a spirit (or better, "Spirit") of wisdom and of revelation in the knowledge of him, having the eyes of your hearts enlightened, that you may know what is the hope to which he has called you, what are the riches of his glorious inheritance in the saints, and what is the immeasurable greatness of his power in us who believe . . ." (1:17-19). This passage unfolds the stages of spiritual progress. It is those who "believe" who experience the fullness of God's power. But first they must "know" its greatness, and for this they need the enlightenment of the heart's eyes by the Holy Spirit.

This, then, is the order: enlightenment, knowledge, faith, experience. It is by enlightenment that we know,

49

and by faith that we enter into the enjoyment of what we know. Our faith-experience is therefore largely conditioned by our heart-knowledge. Further, the more we know, the greater our spiritual capacity becomes and the greater our responsibility to claim our inheritance by faith. Thus, when a person is really born of the Spirit, his grasp of God's purpose for him is usually very limited and his experience is limited in proportion. But as the Holy Spirit enlightens the eyes of his heart, vistas begin to open up before him of which at first he had scarcely even dreamed. He begins to see and know the hope of God's calling, the riches of God's inheritance and the greatness of God's power. He is challenged to embrace by faith the fullness of God's purpose for him. The tragedy is that so often our faith does not keep pace with our knowledge. Our eyes are opened to see more and more of the wonders of God's purpose for us in Christ, but we hang back from appropriating it by faith. This is one of the ways in which we lose the fullness of the Spirit, not necessarily by disobedience but by disbelief. Our lungs develop, but we do not use them. We need constantly to repent of our unbelief and to cry to God to increase our faith, so that, as our knowledge grows, our faith may grow with it and we may continuously lay hold of more of the greatness of God's power and purpose.

We have been considering an empirical objection to our thesis, namely that all Christians cannot have been baptized with the Spirit because they do not seem to have been. Our answer to this objection has been twofold. First, the objector probably has a false *a priori* notion of what the baptism and the fullness of the Spirit involve and therefore of what those baptized and filled should appear to be. We need to assert that neither the baptism nor the fullness of the Spirit need be accompanied by spectacular signs. The initial baptism of the Spirit may be quiet and unsensational, while the continuing fullness of the Spirit manifests itself in moral qualities rather than in miraculous phenomena. Secondly, although our objector is wrong in saying that not all Christians have been baptized with the Spirit, he is right that not all remain filled with the Spirit. We can agree with him in seeking for ourselves and urging upon others an ever growing experience of the Holy Spirit's indwelling fullness.

I turn now to the second category of people mentioned above. There are those today, as there have always been in the Church, to whom the Holy Spirit has given special experiences. The Holy Spirit is God the Lord. He is the divine Spirit, the mighty Spirit; we should not attempt to limit his sovereignty. Although we have sought to discover from the New Testament the Holy Spirit's *norm* for most Christian people, which is one initiatory baptism and a continuous and increasing fullness or repeated fillings, yet we do not deny that he works *abnormally* in some. There are unusual, special operations of the Holy Spirit, notably perhaps in times of revival. Sometimes the bestowing of certain spiritual gifts seems to be accompanied by a quickening, an enriching, a deepening of the recipient's spiritual life. Sometimes a fresh filling with the Holy Spirit, especially after a period of disobedience and declension, may lift the penitent believer suddenly onto an altogether new plane of spiritual life and power.

53

Sometimes the Holy Spirit's inward witness to the believer may be strongly and wonderfully confirmed in his heart, so that he is completely delivered from doubt and darkness. Sometimes the Holy Spirit may come upon a believer to intensify his Christian life in what might be called a personal revival or visitation. Sometimes a Christian worker is given supernatural power for the particular work to which God has called him; he is "anointed," [9] we sometimes say, with special power for special ministry. Sometimes the Holy Spirit may do his distinctively new covenant work of glorifying the Lord Jesus (Jn. 16:14), that is, revealing and manifesting him, in such a way as to make us "rejoice with unutterable and exalted joy" (1 Pet. 1:8). Sometimes the Holy Spirit may even give to the believer what he gave to the apostle Paul, "visions and revelations of the Lord," so that Paul said he was "caught up to the third heaven" and "heard things that cannot be told, which man may not utter" (2 Cor. 12:1-4).

I do not for a moment deny any of these things. Nevertheless, these are not the usual, general, or common purpose of God for all his people, but the unusual, particular, and exceptional ministries of the Holy Spirit to some. Those to whom the sovereign Spirit grants such

[9] *We should use this word cautiously, however, because in one sense all Christian believers have been "anointed" with, or have received the "anointing" of, the Holy Spirit (2 Cor. 1:21, AV; 1 Jn. 2:20, 27).*

54

experiences should indeed bow down and worship God in gratitude. But they should not, if they are true to Scripture, refer to any of them as the baptism of the Spirit. Nor should they urge the same experiences upon others as if they were the spiritual norm. Nor should they suggest that such unusual spiritual experiences are the secret of either holiness or usefulness, since many in the history of the Church have been powerful in character and ministry without them, while the Corinthians, who had some of them, remained carnal.

In conclusion, I take the liberty of issuing some personal and practical exhortations—first to those of us who have received no exceptional manifestation of the Holy Spirit, secondly to those who have, and thirdly to all of us, whatever our experiences may have been.

First, let me address those who have received no unusual experiences of the Holy Spirit. It would be easy for us, through fear or pride or envy, to question or even deny the validity of such experiences. But it would be wrong for us to do so for no better reason than that others claim to have had them, while we have not. We must certainly "test everything" and in particular "test the spirits" (1 Thess. 5:21; 1 Jn. 4:1). We may also feel it wise about some claims to suspend judgment. At the same time, provided that there is nothing in the claimed experience which is contrary to Scripture, and provided that the fruits of the experiences seem to be beneficial to the believer and edifying to the Church, then we must be humbly ready to recognize the unusual operations of the Holy Spirit in others and at least say with Gamaliel: "... let them alone; for if this plan or this undertaking is of men, it will fail; but if it is of God, you will not be able to overthrow them. You might even be found opposing God!" (Acts 5:38, 39) We all need, in these days in which the Holy Spirit seems to be stirring, to be sensitive to what he may be saying and doing among us. We must be very careful neither to blaspheme against the Holy Spirit by attributing his work to the devil, nor to quench the Holy Spirit by resolving to contain him within our own safe, traditional patterns. On the other hand, we should also not manifest a sinful discontent with his *normal* operations in us. Abnormal experiences are not necessary to Christian maturity. We should rejoice in what we do know of the Holy Spirit as teacher and witness, and in the love, joy, peace, and power which he has given us.

Secondly, a word to those who have been given some unusual visitation of the Spirit. You are, of course, thanking God for his great grace vouchsafed to you; but remember that the Holy Spirit is a sovereign Spirit. He not only distributes different spiritual gifts "as he wills" (1 Cor. 12:11), but he exercises his unusual ministries according to his will also. It is understandable that you should want to bear witness to what God has done for you. But I beg you not to seek to stereotype everybody's spiritual experience, nor to imagine that the Holy Spirit necessarily purposes to give to others what he has given to you. It is spiritual *graces* which should be common to all Christians, not spiritual *gifts* or spiritual *experiences*. The gifts of the Spirit are distributed among different Christians (1 Cor. 12); it is the fruit of the Spirit which should characterize all. In a word, let your experience lead you to worship and praise; but let your exhortation to others be grounded not upon your experiences, but upon Scripture. More particularly, I would appeal to you not to urge upon people a baptism with the Spirit as a second and subsequent experience entirely distinct from conversion, for this cannot be proved from Scripture. Instead, please urge upon us what *is* constantly urged in Scripture, namely that we should not grieve nor quench the Holy Spirit (Eph. 4:30; 1 Thess. 5:19), but rather walk in the Spirit and be filled with the Spirit (Gal. 5:16; Eph. 5:18). Urge these things upon us, and we shall be thankful.

Thirdly, an exhortation to us all, whatever our spiritual condition may be. Let us constantly seek to be filled with the Spirit, to be led by the Spirit, to walk in the Spirit. Can we not gladly occupy this common ground together, so that there be no division among us? Further, we can agree that the main condition of being filled is to be hungry. The Scripture tells us that God fills the hungry with good things and sends the rich empty away. "Open your mouth wide," he says, "and I will fill it" (Ps. 81:10). This does not mean that we can ever in this life be filled to hunger no more. Of course, God in Christ through the Spirit does satisfy our hunger and quench our thirst, but it

59

is only of the next life that it is finally written, "They shall hunger no more, neither thirst any more" (Rev. 7:16). In this life our hunger is satisfied only to break out again. Jesus said, "Blessed are those who hunger and thirst for righteousness" (Mt. 5:6), implying that hungering and thirsting after righteousness is as much a permanent state of the Christian as being "poor in spirit" or "meek" or "merciful." So let neither those who have had unusual experiences, nor those who have not, imagine that they have "attained," and that God cannot fill them any fuller with himself! We all need to hear and obey the gracious invitation of Jesus: "If any one thirst, let him come to me and drink." We must learn to keep coming to Jesus, and to keep drinking. Only so, in the wise and balanced language of the Book of Common Prayer, shall we "daily increase in the Holy Spirit more and more, until we come unto God's everlasting kingdom."